Are You A Perfect Dam Leader?

Guide to Self-Assessment and Strategies to Overcoming Perfectionism in Leadership

by
Barbara A. D'Anna, DSL

Bloomington, IN      Milton Keynes, UK
authorHOUSE®

AuthorHouse™
1663 Liberty Drive, Suite 200
Bloomington, IN 47403
www.authorhouse.com
Phone: 1-800-839-8640

AuthorHouse™ UK Ltd.
500 Avebury Boulevard
Central Milton Keynes, MK9 2BE
www.authorhouse.co.uk
Phone: 08001974150

First published by AuthorHouse 9/18/2006

ISBN: 1-4259-4016-1 (sc)

Printed in the United States of America
Bloomington, Indiana

This book is printed on acid-free paper.

To Kurt

Thank you for making my life perfect.

I would like to thank my parents, Anthony & Louise D'Anna, for instilling in me the importance of education and for setting me off on the right path of values and beliefs.

I would also like to thank my in-laws, Vincent & Susan Clemente, for their support and encouragement throughout this project.

I am especially grateful to Dr. Bruce Winston & Dr. Jacque King for their mentoring and guidance in my leadership education and for so willingly sharing their knowledge and expertise.

Last but not least, I would like to thank my children, Kymn, Michael, Danna, Clifford and Barbara, for their patience and tolerance of my parenting efforts and imperfections.

Contents

Introduction

In today's environment, we are bombarded with messages about the importance and ease of improving any flaw. We have come to accept that we must strive for perfection in all aspects of our lives albeit the right laundry detergent for brighter clothes, the right face cream for younger skin or the right education for a successful career. Though out our lives, the concept of being perfect has been re-enforced in the media, at work, in school and by our parents. Therefore, it is both common and natural for leaders to strive to overcome their human imperfections. In reality, no one gets pleasure from making mistakes or exposing their flaws. As a society we have come to accept the notion that 'anything worth doing is worth doing well' and if we can't do it extremely well we are lacking. G.K. Chesterton (1910) says, "A thing worth doing it is worth doing badly" and later adds "the first time."

Overall there is nothing wrong with leaders striving for perfection, neatness, organization or always being on time. In fact achieving this goal can be quite rewarding (adaptive perfectionism). According to Smith (1990) the problem arises when a leader believes that reaching perfection is necessary for self-esteem, peace of mind and acceptance by others (maladaptive perfectionism).

Maladaptive perfectionism (MP) is addicting. The MP leader sets lofty/superhuman goals both for him/herself and his/her followers but even when these goals are reached there is no feeling of satisfaction. This empty feeling causes the leader to work harder, better and longer; setting goals at an ever increasing level of achievement. Like a hamster on a wheel the MP leader is constantly running to achieve the joy of success. They struggle with control issues, lack of intimacy and shared feelings, gaps in levels of emotional growth or recovery and communication.

Perfectionism is neither just good nor bad but rather a continuum that goes from good to bad, from adaptive to maladaptive. There are three factors that influence where one falls on the perfectionism continuum: self-esteem, self-efficacy and narcissism. Just like perfectionism; self-esteem, self-efficacy and narcissism should not be viewed as either good or bad, but rather as a continuum from good to bad.

This book contains four self-assessment surveys (perfectionism, self-esteem, self-efficacy and narcissism) that will help leaders determine where they fall on these continuums and suggests strategies to overcome perfectionism behaviors and beliefs.

The purpose of this book is: to provide leaders with the tools to identify if they are maladaptive perfectionists; to identify the causes of maladaptive perfectionism; and to discuss strategies to overcome maladaptive perfectionism.

The Tale of the Perfect Dam Leader

Once upon the time in the land of Bake Melieve there lived two beavers, Adaper and Malaper, both skilled in building dams. One day the Grand Wizard of Bake Melieve called the two beavers to his palace and told them of his plan to build dams throughout the Kingdom. He, however, was not sure which of the two beavers to hire to construct the dams. Both beavers had impeccable credentials, owned reputable dam construction companies and had been recommended by the Grand Wizard's trusted advisors. The Grand Wizard decided to give both Adaper and Malaper an opportunity to build a dam to help him decide whom to award the lucrative construction contract.

The Grand Wizard asked Adaper if he could construct a dam over the Landycand River in five weeks. Adaper gave this some thought and replied, "Yes, Sire. I will be able to construct a strong and sturdy dam in five weeks." Thinking on his feet, Adaper gave an impromptu presentation on his dam construction philosophy and methods. The Grand Wizard thanked Adaper and remarked, "That was a good presentation." To which Adaper's replied, "Thank you Sire" and smiled with a deep sense of satisfaction.

The Grand Wizard then asked Malaper if he could construct a dam over the Macpan River in five weeks. Malaper immediately replied, "Sire, I can construct two perfect dam in three weeks!" Feeling very self-conscious and unprepared, Malaper gave an impromptu presentation on his perfect dam construction abilities.

The Grand Wizard said "My, how eager and ambitious of you, Malaper, you certainly place a great deal of emphasis on being a perfectionist." To which Malaper replied, "Thank you Sire" and smiled with a sick feeling in his gut that he hadn't put his best foot forward.

And so the Grand Wizard and his advisors conferred and agreed that both dam construction companies would be given five weeks to build a dam, over the assigned rivers. The Grand Wizard and his advisors would then evaluate each dam in order to decide which company should be awarded the contract to build dams throughout the Kingdom.

Adaptive and Maladaptive Perfectionism

As a leader, when you hear someone say, "Wow what a perfect seminar!" or "It was a perfect presentation." you recognize the statement to be a compliment, an expression of extreme satisfaction. Yet when you hear someone say, "He is a perfectionist." you immediately know this is not meant as a compliment but rather as a criticism, a put down. It implies 'he' is overly fussy and nit picks to the extreme of missing the bigger picture by concentrating on the finest of details.

In general, striving for perfection is a good thing; putting forth your best effort and going the extra mile is commendable in all aspects of your life. Perfectionism represents attention to detail, caring about how others view your work and constantly striving to do the very best you can. We all believe that the goal of reaching perfection is both attainable and necessary and will work towards that goal (adaptive perfectionism). In that light, the adaptive perfectionist (AP) leader is able to achieve personal success and experience feelings of satisfaction and accomplishment and the knowledge that his/her best efforts paid off, even if no one notices.

However, when we carry the pursuit of perfection to the extreme and never feel as if things are ever perfect we experience stress and conflict both directly and indirectly (maladaptive perfectionism). The maladaptive perfectionist leader never achieves personal success and experiences feelings of self-doubt, frustration, disappointment, sadness, anger and fear of humiliation.

Perfectionism can be a symptom of some common psychological or psychiatric problems such as obsessive-compulsive disorders, anorexia nervosa, bulimia and/or depression and suicidal tendencies. Perfectionism is linked to physical problems such as abdominal pain, alcoholism, Type A coronary-prone behavior and migraines.

The Focus of Perfectionism

Perfectionism has both an inward (self) and outward (others) focus (Basco, 1999). The inward focus revolves around a self-image of an ugly, stupid, flawed person that can never get anything right. The MPs inward belief is that nothing they do is ever good enough. The outward focus revolves around the image of others as stupid and flawed and incapable of performing satisfactorily. The MPs outward belief is that they are better off doing everything themselves rather than depending on others. Characteristically, MPs have the traits of both an inward and outward focus. They fluidly move between an inward and outward focus depending upon the situation. For example, an MP would be inwardly focused when making a presentation; convinced that he/she had been viewed negatively by the audience. While an outward focus would be associated with a subordinate making a presentation. The MP would be convinced that due to the subordinates 'mistakes' the presentation reflected badly on them and they should just have made the presentation themselves. Herein lies the 'Catch 22'. Whether the MP makes the presentation or delegates it to a subordinate, they are left with feelings of inadequacy and failure.

Therefore, regardless of the situation/focus the MP is afraid to make mistakes and be humiliated by their own actions (inward) or the actions of others associated with them (outward). Another trait common to both foci is the setting of high expectations for self and others. In most cases, these expectations are unrealistic and at the very least difficult to achieve without considerable physical and/or mental stress.

Perfectionism as an Advantage

Perfectionism is a trait that is advantageous for leaders to be successful. An AP leader is generally well-organized and maintains a calm work environment. Their attention to detail results in followers confidence in his/her ability: to make informed decisions, to continually evaluate progress identifying opportunities for improvement and to recognize and attend to all the 'loose ends' associated with a project/job. The AP leader values the opinions of others, welcoming both positive and negative feedback. Their expectation is to see followers do their best by holding them to high standards and encouraging and motivating them to succeed. For example, the AP leader recognizes the followers' abilities and expertise and empowers them to accomplish tasks with minimal supervision.

The AP leader's internal drive for success and personal high standards motivates followers to want to do their best. Followers respect the AP leader's commitment to excellence, value his/her self-confidence and look to the AP leader as a role model.

Perfectionism as a Disadvantage

And while there are advantages associated with being an AP leader, it logically follows that there are disadvantages associated with being an MP leader. In fact, it can be said that an MP leader's drive for success sets him/her up for failure. His/her extreme attention to detail becomes so time consuming that projects literally stall while the leader pursues minutia that would/should otherwise be ignored. Self-doubt prevents the MP leader from making decisions or starting a project. The MP leader must have the right lighting in the room, the proper temperature, and be physically well in order to perform the tasks. He/she becomes so bogged down in details and the need to be perfect that decisions are made as a reaction versus choice or left to just evolve through necessity. The MP leader sets very high standards for self and others. These expectations are usually unrealistic and seldom met. If they are met, the MP leader does not feel personal satisfaction or success but feelings of emptiness (it wasn't good enough; I could have done more/faster/better). There is, however, a craving for the feeling of accomplishment that causes the MP leader to spiral out of control by setting ever increasing expectations (for self and others) further insuring failure. The MP leader is like a hamster in a wheel, running in place until he/she burns out.

The belief that followers cannot be trusted and will take advantage of the leader creates tension in the workplace. The MP leader believes that followers should think and behave exactly as the leader thinks and behaves, nothing else is acceptable. For example, followers are expected to have the same opinion as the leader; any negative or contradictory opinions only fortify the leader's belief that he/she is not perfect and therefore not really accepted by the followers. Followers experience frustration and anger as a result of the MP leader's inability: to make decisions, to seek and value their opinion, and to delegate meaningful work and/or empower them.

Factors Related to Perfectionism

Research done in the area of perfectionism has identified this phenomena as a wide spread problem linked to both physical and psychological disorders. Research associated with leadership has looked specifically at leader behavior, characteristics/traits and relationship with followers. The relationship between leadership and perfectionism is explored in a2003 study by Jacque King, assistant professor in the School of Leadership Studies at regent University. Specifically, this study focuses on leader self-concept in an attempt to understand what motivates the leader to be perfect in all he/she does and says. The study suggests that how a leader views his/her capabilities and self-image can result in a need for power to overcome feelings of inadequacy and fear of humiliation. King suggests that perfectionism (adaptive) in leadership develops out of a desire to do the right thing through discipline, drive and motivation. It is the result of knowing what the right thing to do is and then doing it. Yet perfectionism can be overdone (maladaptive) through control, manipulation and domination.

This raises the question "What causes MP in leaders?" Simply put, genetics and experience are the underlying cause of MP in leaders.

We are born with genetically inherited personality traits that elicit behavioral responses and emotional reactions from us. Overtime these behavior responses and emotional reactions are shaped and/or altered through life experiences. For example, the type of approval we receive from significant people in our lives could alter our course from AP to MP. Conditional approval (you're good, but you could be better) can shape/alter behavior and emotions in such a way that we embark on an endless journey for unconditional approval (you're good). We become conditioned to avoid the pain of criticism and to crave approval. Thus, we strive for perfection by setting ever increasing expectations in order to reach that moment when we are rewarded for doing it to perfection. However, the reward for doing it perfectly is not the prize the MP leader really seeks. He/she really wants to be unconditionally accepted without having to 'do it perfectly' (prove worthiness). The prize the MP leader seeks is acceptance in spite of any imperfections.

Three factors have identified as the underlying elements of MP. These factors are: self-esteem, self-efficacy and narcissism. Each factor will be discussed separately in the following sections.

Tale of the Perfect Dam Leader – Week One

Adaper eagerly called together his team of workers and shared with them the Grand Wizards plan. They spent the next few hours brainstorming how best to proceed with the construction of the dam over the Landycand River. Adaper suggested using oak leaves and twigs and mud from the river bank. Some members of the team disagreed and suggested that while oak leaves and twigs would be good filler; silt, from the bottom of the river rather than mud, would provide a sturdier base for the dam. Adaper turned this suggestion over in his mind. "Hmmm," he thought, "what a smart team I have, this is a great idea."

Adaper worked with his team to develop a project plan. Tasks and responsibilities were identified and assigned to each of the team members. Adaper left the meeting confident that his team had the ability to get the job done. The team left the meeting motivated to do their best for Adaper. They agreed to meet again in one week to review their progress.

Across town, Malaper sat alone in his office and thought about how best to start the dam project. He thought, "I could use maple leaves and oak twigs and mud from the river bank, but, no, that wouldn't be good enough. Hmmmm, perhaps I should use pebbles from the river bottom and maple twigs and silt. He was sure that if he made a mistake and the dam wasn't perfect, he would be humiliated. As he reorganized the papers on his desk (for the seventh time), Malaper thought about the Grand Wizards comment referring to him as eager and ambitious. He was sure that it was meant as a criticism and implied that Malaper was not a capable dam builder. He felt the flush of anger at having to agree to building one dam in five weeks. He knew that he could construct two perfect dams in three weeks; just as he knew that reaching this lofty goal would bring him great acclaim.

Malaper continued to obsess about how to start the project for the greater part of week one. Towards the end of the week, his workers, having heard rumor of the dam project, went to Malaper's office. "Mr. Malaper," they asked, "what plans have you made for this project?"

Malaper, feeling challenged, reacted by reiterating the last plan that had crossed his mind. "I have decided to construct the dam using pebbles from the river bottom, maple leaves, oak twigs and a mixture of silt from the bottom of the river and mud from the river bank." The team of workers looked perplexed; certainly this was overkill for dam construction. One brave worker spoke up. "It would be more efficient, practical and less expensive to go with a simpler mix such as maple leaves and twigs and mud."

Malaper didn't understand why his workers didn't always see things the way he did. Clearly, he was the expert and they were lacking in ability and knowledge. Malaper steadied his gaze on the brave worker and snapped, "Do you know anything about dam construction? Apparently not! This dam needs to be perfect, no mistakes and if I go with your suggestions the dam will be a failure." And so will I, he thought. "I'm the perfect dam leader and my plan is the one that will be followed. Tension began to build in the room.

Malaper spent the rest of the day dictating the details of the plan to the workers; where the pebbles should be found, their size, color and texture; what company to get the leaves and twigs from, their size, color and texture etc. Tasks and responsibilities were assigned and they planned to meet in week two to review their progress.

Both Malaper and the team of workers left the meeting feeling frustrated.

Perfectionism Self-Assessment Survey

Do you have difficulties with perfectionism? Take the following self-assessment to identify where you are on the perfection continuum and what/if changes are needed.

The Perfectionism Self-Assessment Survey is the first of four self-assessment tools included in this book. The three remaining self-assessment tools are designed to address the factors that influence perfectionism: self-esteem, self-efficacy and narcissism. You will encounter the three remaining surveys in the sections devoted to self-esteem, self-efficacy and narcissism respectively.

To identify if you are an adaptive perfectionist or a maladaptive perfectionist complete the Perfectionism Self-Assessment Survey that follows. Because we are sometimes unable to be as objective as we should be, it is recommended that you ask someone you trust to rate you using the Self-Assessment Survey. Compare your answers and discuss any discrepancies.

Barbara A. D'Anna, DSL

Perfectionism Self-Assessment Survey

(Frost, 1990)

Indicate your level of agreement with the following statements using a five- point Likert scale:
1: Strongly Disagree, 2: Disagree, 3: Neutral, 4: Agree, 5: Strongly Agree

1. Even when things are tough, I can perform quite well.

   Strongly Disagree   Strongly Agree

   1___   2___   3___   4___   5___

2. I am very good at focusing my efforts on attaining a goal.

   Strongly Disagree   Strongly Agree

   1___   2___   3___   4___   5___

3. If I fail partly, it is as bad as being a complete failure.

   Strongly Disagree   Strongly Agree

   1___   2___   3___   4___   5___

4. Only outstanding performance is good enough for me.

   Strongly Disagree   Strongly Agree

   1___   2___   3___   4___   5___

5. A significant person in my life has set very high standards for me.

   Strongly Disagree   Strongly Agree

   1___   2___   3___   4___   5___

6. People will probably think less of me if I make a mistake.

   Strongly Disagree   Strongly Agree

   1___   2___   3___   4___   5___

7. At sometime in y life, I was punished for not doing things perfectly.

   Strongly Disagree   Strongly Agree

   1___   2___   3___   4___   5___

8. I wish I could have more respect for myself.

    Strongly Disagree   Strongly Agree

    1___   2___   3___   4___   5___

9. A significant person in my life never tried to understand my mistakes.

    Strongly Disagree   Strongly Agree

    1___   2___   3___   4___   5___

10. I certainly feel useless at times.

    Strongly Disagree   Strongly Agree

    1___   2___   3___   4___   5___

11. I tend to get behind in my work because I repeat things over and over.

    Strongly Disagree   Strongly Agree

    1___   2___   3___   4___   5___

12. At times I think I am no good at all.

    Strongly Disagree   Strongly Agree

    1___   2___   3___   4___   5___

13. I try to be an organized person.

    Strongly Disagree   Strongly Agree

    1___   2___   3___   4___   5___

14. All in all, I am inclined to feel that I am a failure.

    Strongly Disagree   Strongly Agree

    1___   2___   3___   4___   5___

15. If I fail at work, I am a failure as a person.

    Strongly Disagree   Strongly Agree

    1___   2___   3___   4___   5___

16. I am confident that I can perform effectively in many different tasks.

    Strongly Disagree   Strongly Agree

    1___   2___   3___   4___   5___

17. I should be upset if I make a mistake.

Strongly Disagree   Strongly Agree

1___   2___   3___   4___   5___

18. I feel I do not have much to be proud of.

Strongly Disagree   Strongly Agree

1___   2___   3___   4___   5___

19. A significant person in my life wanted me to be the best at everything.

Strongly Disagree   Strongly Agree

1___   2___   3___   4___   5___

20. I set higher goals than most people.

Strongly Disagree   Strongly Agree

1___   2___   3___   4___   5___

21. If someone does a task at work better than I, then I feel like I failed the whole

task.

Strongly Disagree   Strongly Agree

1___   2___   3___   4___   5___

22. I always know what I am doing.

Strongly Disagree   Strongly Agree

1___   2___   3___   4___   5___

23. I rarely depend on anyone else to get things done.

Strongly Disagree   Strongly Agree

1___   2___   3___   4___   5___

24. Everyone likes to hear my stories.

Strongly Disagree   Strongly Agree

1___   2___   3___   4___   5___

25. I will never be satisfied until I get all that I deserve.

Strongly Disagree   Strongly Agree

1___   2___   3___   4___   5___

26. Even when I do something very carefully, I often feel that it is not quite right.

Strongly Disagree   Strongly Agree

1___   2___   3___   4___   5___

27. I hate being less than best at things.

Strongly Disagree   Strongly Agree

1___   2___   3___   4___   5___

28. I never felt I could meet my parents' expectations.

Strongly Disagree   Strongly Agree

1___   2___   3___   4___   5___

29. If I do not do as well as other people, it means that I am an inferior human being.

Strongly Disagree   Strongly Agree

1___   2___   3___   4___   5___

30. A significant person in my life always had higher expectations for my future than I have.

Strongly Disagree   Strongly Agree

1___   2___   3___   4___   5___

31. Other people seem to accept lower standards from themselves than I do.

Strongly Disagree   Strongly Agree

1___   2___   3___   4___   5___

32. I usually have doubts about the simple everyday things.

Strongly Disagree   Strongly Agree

1___   2___   3___   4___   5___

33. I expect higher performance in daily tasks than most people.

Strongly Disagree   Strongly Agree

   1___   2___   3___   4___   5___

34. A significant person in my life expected excellence from me.

Strongly Disagree   Strongly Agree

   1___   2___   3___   4___   5___

35. I have a strong will for power.

Strongly Disagree   Strongly Agree

   1___   2___   3___   4___   5___

Scoring the Perfectionism Self-Assessment Survey

Add up the scores for all thirty five items. For example: for each question that you scored as 1(strongly disagree) add 1 point; for each question that you scored as 3 (neutral) add 3 points etc.

Strongly Disagree   Strongly Agree

   1 x___   2 x___   3 x__   4 x___   5 x___

Totals ____ + ____ + ____ + ____ + _____ = _____

                                                        Total Score

If your score 70 or less, you are probably not a maladaptive perfectionist, although you may have a few of the traits. You recognize and accept that you are not perfect. Errors and flaws are viewed as opportunities and are addressed realistically in a manner that fits the situation. You value and seek out the opinions of others, set realistic and achievable goals and derive satisfaction when the job/task is complete. You are probably neat, organized and pay attention to detail; but not to extremes.

Scores from 71- 105 suggest mild maladaptive perfectionism. In general you accept that you are not perfect, however, you have a somewhat exaggerated perception of errors and flaws and the appropriate actions to correct them. For the most part you value the opinion of others, but there are times when their opinions make you feel criticized. You constantly strive to do your best but often feel you are falling short of your goal. You are probably mildly compulsive about neatness, organization and attention to detail.

Scores of 106- 140 suggest moderate maladaptive perfectionism. Your perfectionism tendencies are probably causing you trouble in some areas, but is not out of control. You do not always welcome the opinions of others and question their motivation. Opinions that are not aligned with yours leave you with feelings of self-doubt and rejection. Stress may cause your perfectionism tendencies to increase such that you may react to the situation/problem rather then making choices. Under stress your tendency is to move from self-confidence to self-doubt, all in an effort to avoid feelings of failure and/or humiliation and to maintain a sense of control. Maintaining control is very important to you because giving it up will result in something bad happening. You probably approach neatness, organization and attention to detail with some extreme.

Scores of 141 or higher suggest a high level of maladaptive perfectionism that could cause you serious problems. You are intolerant of people who do things differently than you do and continually criticize anyone who thinks, does and/or verbalize anything that deviates from your standards. You are involved in an endless struggle to achieve high standards in light of your mindset that no effort is ever good enough. You struggle with the fear of making mistakes and humiliation. You are probably neat, organized and pay attention to deal to such excess that you stall projects and miss deadlines. You anticipate the future will be negative and filled with stressful mistakes leaving you with a sense of hopelessness, depression and anxiety.

Tale of the Perfect Dam Leader – Week Two

Adaper's team met to review the progress they were making on the dam project. Adaper determined that arrangements had been made to purchase the required supplies and that they were to be delivered to the dam construction site by week's end. The dam project deadline identified that construction would start week three and be completed by week five. After a review of all the details, the team agreed that they were on schedule.

Adaper thanked his team and told them how great it was to work with such capable and knowledgeable dam builders. The team left the meeting feeling confident and motivated to do their best for Adaper. They eagerly agreed to meet in week three at the construction site.

While across town, Malaper's team met to review the progress they were making on the dam project. Malaper went through an exhaustive checklist of details to be accomplished. He nitpicked about details that were of little to no concern to the projects success. Malaper questioned each of the team members about quality and quantity of supplies ordered. In the end it was determined that arrangements had been made to purchase the required supplies and delivery was set for the end of the week. Malaper knew that had he made the supply arrangements himself, they would have already been delivered to the site.

The dam project timeline was reviewed. And while the team felt confident that they would be able to start the project on week three and complete it by the end of week five; Malaper felt this was not good enough. His inner voice reminded him of his tendency to be lazy and slow. He decided to change the deadline, informing the team that he wanted the dam construction completed by week four. They expressed concern that this was an unrealistic deadline. But Malaper simply reminded them that he was the perfect dam leader and things would be done his way.

Malaper arranged to meet with each of the team members separately to again assure that the details of the supplies being gathered were perfect. He didn't trust the team to get the job done to his specifications and preferred to do things himself rather than delegate. The workers left the meeting anxious about meeting the revised deadline and angry about being micromanaged. They reluctantly agreed to meet at the construction site in week three.

Self-Esteem

This section discusses how self-esteem influences perfectionism and includes a self-assessment survey.

Self-esteem reflects our opinions of ourselves. Therefore, healthy self-esteem can be viewed as a positive acceptance of an accurate and honest self-image. Moreover, low self-esteem and high self-esteem can be viewed as self-defeating and as an exaggerated view of self. Our sense of self is developed from how we are accepted by others. For example, children with healthy self-esteem have parents that value and respect them as individuals and model healthy self-esteem. These parents are consistent, loving, encouraging and express an interest in their children's lives. They do not use shame and/or humiliation as disciplinary tools. Children with unhealthy self-esteem have needy parents who force standards and preferences on them. These parents inconsistently express love and acceptance for 'good' behaviors and consistently express disdain and humiliation for 'bad' behaviors. This parenting style lays the foundation for low self-esteem in children by creating an image of self as being inferior, stupid and bad. Children have the choice to believe that what they do is bad or that they are bad. Children with low self-esteem believe that they are bad and thus worthless.

Throughout our lives we reinforce the early lessons of acceptance by developing an internal voice that will continue the critical and demeaning messages, programmed by parents and other authority figures, that reaffirm a worthless self-image and an inability to be successful. For example, if a MP accidentally drops a glass and breaks it, the inner voice will admonishes him/her by saying, "I'm stupid and clumsy. I always make a mess out of things."

Leaders with healthy self-esteem are able to acknowledge their weaknesses and simultaneously accept/like themselves. They are able to confront life without fear and to recognize and problem solve without needless worry.

Both low self-esteem and high self-esteem can be viewed as unhealthy. Leaders with low self-esteem develop a painful self-consciousness, which keeps their focus inward inhibiting their ability to enjoy life. For some leaders, low self-esteem is an advantage. It gives them permission to avoid risks, have no expectations, set low goals and be lazy. They believe that by doing nothing they will rarely disappoint themselves or others.

Leaders with high self-esteem are also focused inwardly and unable to enjoy life. However, this is not because of a painful self-consciousness but from a sense of arrogance. Low self-esteem and high self-esteem create a sense of fear of failure and insecurity in leaders. This fear of failure is the catalyst for setting unrealistically high expectations in an effort to achieve 'perfectionism'.

Self-Esteem Assessment Survey

(Rosenberg, 1965)

Indicate your level of agreement with the following statements using a five- point Likert scale:
1: Strongly Disagree, 2: Disagree, 3: Neutral, 4: Agree, 5: Strongly Agree

1. I fell that I am a person of worth, at least on an equal plane with others.

    Strongly Disagree   Strongly Agree

    1___   2___   3___   4___   5___

2. I will be able to achieve most of the goals that I have set for myself.

    Strongly Disagree   Strongly Agree

    1___   2___   3___   4___   5___

3. It is important that I be thoroughly competent in everything that I do.

    Strongly Disagree   Strongly Agree

    1___   2___   3___   4___   5___

4. I take a positive attitude towards myself.

    Strongly Disagree   Strongly Agree

    1___   2___   3___   4___   5___

5. When facing difficult tasks. I am certain that I will accomplish them.

    Strongly Disagree   Strongly Agree

    1___   2___   3___   4___   5___

6. I feel that I have a number of good qualities.

    Strongly Disagree   Strongly Agree

    1___   2___   3___   4___   5___

7. Organization is very important to me.

    Strongly Disagree   Strongly Agree

    1___   2___   3___   4___   5___

8. I will be able to successfully overcome my challenges.

    Strongly Disagree   Strongly Agree

    1___   2___   3___   4___   5___

9. I have extremely high goals.

    Strongly Disagree   Strongly Agree

    1___   2___   3___   4___   5___

10. If I do not do well all the time, people will not respect me.

    Strongly Disagree   Strongly Agree

    1___   2___   3___   4___   5___

Scoring the Self-Esteem Survey

Add up the scores on all ten items. For example: for each question that you scored as 1(strongly disagree) add 1 point; for each question that you scored as 3 (neutral) add 3 points etc.

Strongly Disagree   Strongly Agree

    1 x___   2 x___   3 x___   4 x___   5 x___

Totals ____   +   ____   +   ____   +   ____   +   _____   =   _____

                                                         Total Score

Scores of 1- 20 suggest you hold an unrealistic and unappreciative opinion of yourself. Your probably view of self is that of inferiority to others. You operate from a position of submission. Your lack of self- respect is viewed by others as incompetence. You are apathetic, set very low goals and have no expectations of yourself.

Scores of 21-39 suggest you hold a realistic opinion of yourself. Your probably view of self is that of being equal to others. You are able to achieve pleasure from your achievements and talents, while recognizing your imperfections and opportunities for growth. You operate from a position of self-respect and dignity, usually have a calm demeanor and are not easily angered. You are glad to be who you are.

Scores of 40 or higher suggests you hold an arrogant, pretentious opinion of yourself. Your probably view of self is that of superiority to others. You operate from a position of fear and insecurity. You regularly employ an air of infallibility as a mechanism of defense. You have an excessive need to be admired.

Tale of the Perfect Dam Leader – Week Three

Adaper's team met as scheduled at the construction site. The required supplies were all there with the exception of the oak leaves. The leaf company reported, due to high demand, the leaves were temporarily out of stock and would be shipped by the end of week four. The team discussed the situation and decided that the project would be delayed if they waited for the oak leaves to be shipped. They contacted the leaf company, identified that elm leaves were readily available, and they could be delivered to the construction site the next day. They conferred and agreed that elm leaves were an acceptable substitute and placed the order.

The team reviewed the project plans, the assigned tasks and responsibilities and their progress. Adaper thanked the team members for their good work and efforts. They team members in turn told Adaper that he was a great leader and working with and for him was a pleasure.

They agreed to meet week four at the construction site.

Malaper's team met week three at the construction site. The required supplies were all there with the exception of half of the pebbles from the bottom of the river. The pebble company reported that, due to demand, river bottom pebbles were temporarily out of stock, and could be delivered by week four. Upon hearing this news, Malaper flew into a rage. He ranted, "If you want things done right you have to do them yourself." He contacted the pebble company and was informed that there were ample pebbles from the forest floor available. Again, he ranted, "this would not do, it must be perfect, the project would not fail." He thought to himself, "I will not fail." The team suggested using the pebbles from the forest floor as the change would not alter the sturdiness of the dam and that waiting for the pebbles from the river bed would cause them to miss the revised week four deadline and might cause them to miss the original week five deadline. "No! No! No!" raged Malapers. "That will not do, the dam project must be perfect! Nothing else is acceptable!" He told the team that he would handle the situation to insure no further screw ups. He also reminded the team that he was a perfect dam leader and as such he still expected a perfect dam to be constructed week four.

The team members muttered to themselves, "What he means is my way or the highway. What a jerk!" There was palpable tension in the air.

Malaper told the workers the next meeting was scheduled for week four.

Self-Efficacy

This section discusses how self-efficacy influences perfectionism and includes a self-assessment survey.

Self-efficacy is our individual beliefs about our abilities to perform effectively. For example, it is whether or not the leader believes he/she has the abilities and/or capabilities to lead. More specifically, self-efficacy is not the number of skills a leader has but what the leader believes he/she can accomplish under a variety of circumstances. In fact, the very aspiration to rise to a leadership position is the product of efficacious beliefs.

We tend to confuse self-efficacy (act) with the actual performance (outcome). It is important to recognize that the actual performance is a consequence of efficacious beliefs and not part of the beliefs. The act produces the outcome. For example, the leader believes (act) he/she has the capabilities to perform a specific task. He/she then applies these capabilities to the situation which results in a successful performance (outcome). It is conceivable that different leaders with similar skills or the same leader under different circumstances could demonstrate performance fluctuations (fail/succeed) depending on his/her efficacious beliefs.

Self-efficacy is influenced by feedback and experience. Throughout life our 'performance' is repeatedly evaluated and conveyed to us both directly and indirectly. Informally, we receive comments about the causes of our successes and failures as well our performance is compared to that of others. Formally, we are evaluated against established sets of criteria. It logically follows that being told that we have demonstrated abilities in our performance results in high self-efficacy. While, the converse is also true; being told that we lack the abilities to perform results in low self-efficacy. The experience of repeatedly not being able to successfully perform/complete a task influences the level of self-efficacy. For example, if you were to bake a cheesecake everyday for a year and each attempt resulted in uneatable runny goop; you would come away from the experience believing that you lack the abilities needed to bake cheesecakes. However, if you come away from the experience with the notion that you will succeed if you set higher standards and intensify and persist in your efforts you may be crossing the line into maladaptive perfectionism.

Self-Efficacy Survey

(Chen, Gully & Eden, 2001)

Indicate your agreement with the following statements by checking either Yes or No.

1. I have natural talent for influencing people.

    Yes_____   No_____

2. Modesty doesn't become me.

    Yes_____   No_____

3. I would do almost anything on a dare.

    Yes_____   No_____

4. I know I am good because everyone keeps telling me so.

    Yes_____   No_____

5. If I ruled the world it would be a better place.

    Yes_____   No_____

6. I can usually talk my way out of anything.

    Yes_____   No_____

7. I like to be the center of attention.

    Yes_____   No__

8. I will be a success.

    Yes_____   No_____

9. I think I am a special person.

    Yes_____   No_____

10. I see myself as a good leader.

    Yes_____   No_____

Scoring the Self-Efficacy Survey

Total the number of Yes answers.

Total Score_____

If your score is 1-5, you probably do not believe you can perform successfully. Your tendency is to expect to fail. This tendency causes you to quit trying (give up) prematurely.

Scores of 6-10 suggests a belief in your ability to perform successfully. Your expectation of success causes you to exert the effort needed to overcome any and all obstacles to completion of a project/task.

Tale of the Perfect Dam Leader – Week Four

Adaper meets with his team as scheduled. The substitute elm leaves have been arrived and the project proceeds as scheduled. A review of the timeline identified that the strong and sturdy dam would be completed in week five and if things continued to hum along completion is possible by the end of week four. Adaper and the team celebrated their success and looked forward to the dam evaluation by the Grand Wizard and his advisors.

Malaper meets with his workers as scheduled. The pebbles from the river bed were delivered and the project finally started. From an exhausted review of the timeline it was evident that the perfect dam would not be constructed by week four and might not be completed by week five. Malaper silently berated himself for not completing the dam project by week four totally disregarding the fact that the Grand Wizard's deadline was week five. He was angry and felt that the team was incompetent and lazy and had taken advantage of him. They always made him look bad in front of customers. He vowed not to forget their mistakes and would include statements about their incompetence on their annual evaluations.

The workers were both frustrated and angry. They were, however, determined to complete the project on time for their personal satisfaction.

Malaper dreaded meeting with The Grand Wizard and his advisors for the dam evaluation. He was experiencing self-doubt, frustration, fear of humiliation and failure.

Narcissism

This section discusses how narcissism influences perfectionism and includes a self-assessment survey.

Freud defined narcissism as "perfection" but in reality it is the illusion of perfection. The fear of failure and humiliation causes the creation of a narcissistic fantasy of perfection. For example, individuals will create grandiose fantasies of success and adoration to protect themselves from feelings of self-doubt and a lack of self-confidence.

The narcissistic personality is developed in early childhood as a result of a conflict-marked relationship with parents; specifically, when parents send messages of conditional love and acceptance. For example, parents will hold a child to an idealized image of brilliance and will shower that child with affection and praise when the child performs up to this image but will be critical and outraged when the child fails to perform 'brilliantly'. Children then grow to realize that acceptance, admiration and love are conditional upon performance. Therefore, they create grandiose fantasies where they are powerful, successful and adored in an effort to protect themselves from feelings of self-doubt and a lack of confidence.

These grandiose fantasies are the illusion of perfection or the delusion of a glorious self-image. As well, they are the repression of self-loathing and esteem building. Along with the illusion of perfection is the need to dominate.

Dominance provides the narcissist with an outlet for pent-up anger and it enhances self-esteem and reinforces the pursuit of grandiose fantasies.

The narcissistic leader will employ bullying, exploitation and manipulation as needed to maintain their dominate presence. For example, when this leader feels challenged, he/she is prone to uncontrolled ranting and raving to bolster their confidence and destroy the perceived challenger. In general, the narcissistic leader rejects the status quo, doesn't respect or seek the opinions of others and is obsessed with personal image and goals. He/she is very much like the leader with high self-esteem in that they share an arrogance that keeps them focused inward and an exaggerated fear of failure. This fear of failure causes the narcissist to set unrealistically high expectations in the pursuit of 'perfection'.

Narcissism drives people to seek out leadership positions. These leaders are seen as driven 'personalities' who want, can and will change the world. However, underneath the constant smiling face of the narcissistic leader is a fear of humiliation that can have a devastating impact on organizations and subordinates.

Narcissism Self-Assessment Survey

(Raskin & Terry, 1998)

Indicate your level of agreement with the following statements using a five- point Likert scale:
1: Strongly Disagree, 2: Disagree, 3: Neutral, 4: Agree, 5: Strongly Agree

1. I am a neat person.

    Strongly Disagree   Strongly Agree

       1___   2___   3___   4___   5___

2. On the whole I am satisfied with myself.

    Strongly Disagree   Strongly Agree

       1___   2___   3___   4___   5___

3. In general, I think I can obtain outcomes that are important to me.

    Strongly Disagree   Strongly Agree

       1___   2___   3___   4___   5___

4. Neatness is very important to me.

    Strongly Disagree   Strongly Agree

       1___   2___   3___   4___   5___

5. The fewer mistakes I make, the more people will like me.

    Strongly Disagree   Strongly Agree

       1___   2___   3___   4___   5___

6. I believe that I can succeed at any endeavor to which I set my mind.

    Strongly Disagree   Strongly Agree

       1___   2___   3___   4___   5___

7.I am able to do things as well as most people.

    Strongly Disagree   Strongly Agree

       1___   2___   3___   4___   5___

8. Compared to most people, I can do most tasks very well.

Strongly Disagree   Strongly Agree

1___   2___   3___   4___   5___

9. If I do not set the highest standards for myself, I am likely to end up a second rate person.

Strongly Disagree   Strongly Agree

1___   2___   3___   4___   5___

10. I try to be a neat person.

Strongly Disagree   Strongly Agree

1___   2___   3___   4___   5___

11. I never felt I could meet my parents' standards.

Strongly Disagree   Strongly Agree

1___   2___   3___   4___   5___

Scoring the Narcissism Self-Assessment Survey

Add up the scores on all ten items. For example: for each question that you scored as 1(strongly disagree) add 1 point; for each question that you scored as 3 (neutral) add 3 points etc.

Strongly Disagree   Strongly Agree

1 x___   2 x___   3 x___   4 x___   5 x___

Totals   ____   +   ____   +   ____   +   ____   +   ____   =   _____

Total Score

If your score is 22 or less you are probably open to and solicitous of the opinions of others, you can be insensitive and intolerant of criticism at times. You want to be admired and are driven by a need for accomplishment; putting the organization's needs first and your personal needs second. In general, your vision is ambitious and challenging and focuses on achievements for the common good and cooperative action. Your confidence in your skills and abilities and recognition of your limitations allows you to surround yourself with competent people. You have a genuine concern for others and are able to inspire, energize and motivate them. However, your concern for others does take a back seat to achieving your goals. You are able to see the big picture, make decisions and are an excellent delegator. You will occasional use manipulation as a tool to ensure your goals are met.

Scores of 23- 43 suggests that you are cautious and detailed oriented and have a strong fear of failure. This fear causes you to take enormous amounts of time to analyze opportunities and treats, to the point of becoming almost paralytic in the decision making process. You are driven by a need for love rather than glory and want to be thought of with affection. In general, your vision is conservative with an emphasis on analysis and preparation. While you have little concern for others, you believe it is important to present yourself as if you have a great concern for others. A fragile sense of self- worth causes you to surround yourself with weak subordinates who adore you. And although you are willing to accept some criticism from subordinates, you will hold a grudge when you feel betrayed. You will use manipulation as a tool to offset perceived traitors.

Scores of 44 or higher suggests you are probably oversensitive to criticism, don't listen to anyone and have a tendency to exaggerate to the point of lying. You are driven by a need for glory and have a pathological obsession with you image. You view yourself as a savior and demand/ expect hero worship by all. In general, your vision is reckless and only represents your personal goals. Your sense of over confidence allows no time for details or detail analysis, causing you to vacillate between loose delegation and micromanagement. You have absolutely no concern for others and view all subordinates as potential threats. When you fell challenged you fly into uncontrolled fits of rage. Manipulation is just another tool for you.

Tale of the Perfect Dam Leader – Week Five

Adaper and his team arrived early to survey the strong and sturdy dam they has constructed over the Landycand River. They congratulated each other on their successful completion of the dam.

The Grand Wizard and his advisors inspected Adaper's dam and were very pleased and impressed. The Grand Wizard congratulated and praised Adaper for the excellent job. Adaper informed the Grand Wizard that the team deserved the praise for successfully constructing the dam. The Grand Wizard beamed and said, "Adaper, you are a good dam leader."

Malaper's team worked all night long in an attempt to meet the five week deadline. At sunrise, Malaper arrived to survey the completed dam. He ranted and raved at his workers for making him look bad in the eyes of the Grand Wizard.

When the Grand Wizard and his advisors arrived, they were surprised to see that the dam construction was not complete and they expressed this to Malaper. Malaper replied that he did not understand the Grand Wizards surprise after all Malaper had set such high standards and was working with such incompetence, how he could possibly be successful. Clearly, to have met the deadline Adaper must have set lower expectations. A fair man, the Grand Wizard noted how hard the team was working and granted them a one week extension to complete the dam project.

Strategies to Overcome Maladaptive Perfectionism

This section contains a series of exercises that will help you further identify and understand the nature and extent of your perfectionism. Also included in this section are suggested strategies for changing perfectionism behaviors and beliefs.

Perfectionism beliefs and behaviors manifest differently from person to person. Therefore, before beginning to look at the strategies to overcome maladaptive perfectionism either as a potential problem or as a real difficulty, you will need to further clarify what influences/issues are affecting your leadership abilities.

Identifying Behaviors & Beliefs

Behaviors and beliefs driven by perfection differ from person to person due to age situation and cultural orientation. The purpose of the followings exercise is to identify the unique way perfectionism is manifested in you.

Begin by recording the results of the four self-assessment surveys taken in sections 5, 7, 9 and 11. Because, it is hard at times to have an objective/realistic perspective when evaluating yourself, it is recommended that you ask someone you trust to complete the series of exercises from their perspective of you. You should compare answers and discuss the differences.

The Perfectionism Self-Assessment Survey identified my level of perfectionism as: _____

The factor (s) that influence my level of perfectionism are:

Self-Esteem _____   Self- Efficacy_____   Narcissism_____

The four surveys scoring results suggests behaviors and beliefs that you may recognize in myself. However, if you feel that the behaviors and beliefs identified in the four surveys are not reflective of you or if you want further validation of the behaviors/beliefs identified, it is recommended that you keep a diary of perfectionism behaviors and beliefs for two weeks. Each diary entry should include: the situation and the perfectionism behavior and the belief associated with the behavior.

Example

Situation: Meeting with the executive team.

Behavior: Always arrive fifteen minutes before the meeting starts and get angry when others are even a few minutes late.

Belief: It is expected that everyone will arrive fifteen minutes early for meetings. It is not acceptable to be even a few minutes late.

Next, list the behaviors and beliefs that you recognize in yourself (from surveys and/or diary). For each behavior identify the belief associated with it and for each belief identify a behavior associated with it. Estimate to what degree each behavior and belief is a problem for you. For example: not a problem, mild problem, moderate problem or big problem.

Example

Behavior: I do not welcome the opinions of others and question their motivation.

Belief: There is no regard for my knowledge/expertise. They are trying to discredit and/or embarrass me.

Degree: moderate problem

Behaviors & Beliefs Identification Worksheet

Behavior: _____

Belief: _____

Degree: _____

Behavior: _____

Belief: _____

Degree: _____

Behavior: _____

Belief: _____

Degree: _____

Behavior: _____

Belief: _____

Degree: _____

The Impact on Others

Perfectionism behaviors and beliefs can have an adverse impact on others causing tension and frustration both in the workplace and at home. The next exercise will identify the affect your perfectionism behaviors and beliefs have on those around you.

For each of the recognized behaviors and beliefs you listed above answer the following questions.

How do people react when I behavior this way?

How do people respond when I impose my beliefs on them?

How has this behavior/belief affected my relationships?

Who are the people my behavior/beliefs have impacted?

If you feel comfortable, ask the people identified to answer the following questions.

How are you affected when I behavior this way?

What behaviors and/or beliefs would you like to see me change?

Take a few minutes to review and consider the responses to the above questions. Then answer the following question.

How do you feel about the effect your behavior/belief has on others?

Impact on You

As discussed previously, maladaptive perfectionism can cause anxiety, fear, intense angry and depression. The purpose of this exercise is to identify the impact your behaviors and beliefs have on your emotional health.

For this exercise: identify a situation when you have displayed the recognized behaviors and beliefs and how you felt in that situation. For example, anxious, angry, sad, etc.

Example

Behavior/Belief: Organization and neatness are paramount to my success and my being viewed as successful.

Situation: Throughout the day I organize and re-organize the papers on my desk. I can not leave at the end of the day unless I'm sure everything is in its' place.

Emotion: Frustrated

Emotional Impact Identification Worksheet

Behavior/Belief: _____

Situation: _____

Emotion: _____

Behavior/Belief: _____

Situation: _____

Emotion: _____

Behavior/Belief: _____

Situation: _____

Emotion: _____

Behavior/Belief: _____

Situation: _____

Emotion: _____

Plan for Change

Now that you have further identified and better understand the nature and extent of your perfectionism you need to develop a plan for change. As a leader, you know that a plan starts with goal identification that can be used to measure success. The goals need to be specific, realistic and achievable and not driven by perfectionism. Using the information you have gathered thus far, identify your goals.

Example

Goal: Become more tolerant of others:

Allow my co-workers to express their opinions without any displays of anger on my part.

Learn to tolerate questions about projects/decisions I have suggested.

Stop caring how others view me.

Take a few minutes to review the goals and begin to prioritize them. Prioritize the goals based on how important each is to you and identify if it is a short term (achievable in a few month or less) or a long term (achievable in 6 months or more). Remember that the priorities may change as you work though the needed behavior and belief changes.

Changing Beliefs

This section discusses and demonstrates employing the strategies of belief journaling, education and hypothesis testing to change perfectionism beliefs.

The difficulty with changing perfectionist beliefs is two fold, first: you have already made the assumption that your beliefs are appropriate and second: you may have beliefs that you are not aware of because they are located in your unconscious thoughts. The way to overcome these difficulties is to concentrate on identifying situations (rather than beliefs) associated with feelings of not living up to your standards, feelings that others are not living up to your standards and engaging in excessive behaviors (checking and rechecking your work repeatedly).

Belief Journaling

One strategy to change perfectionism beliefs is belief journaling. Belief journaling is a four step process that causes you to analyze your beliefs. The four steps of belief journaling are: belief identification, alternative belief identification, weighing the pro's and con's of the belief and identification of a more realistic belief. A sample diary page follows for you to use for this exercise. However, you can use any format that works for you as long as you include all four components/steps.

Belief Journal Example

Situation: My assistant was fifteen minutes late for a meeting with the executive team.

Belief: He/she is not living up to my standard. Always be on time, no excuses. His/her lateness reflects on me. It made me look bad.

Alternative beliefs:

It is OK for people to be late sometimes

The first fifteen minutes of the meeting are devoted to

pleasantries; nothing of importance is discussed.

My assistant is a dependable person. I can count on him/her.

Weighing Pros & Cons:

The expectation that my assistant should never be late only causes me to be angry and frustrated. It did not change the situation.

Even though he/she was late, my assistant arrived before the agenda was discussed. He/she was prepared to present the appropriate data.

If I trusted that he/she would arrive and be well prepared, I could have relaxed and enjoyed the pre-meeting discussion.

Just because I am early for everything doesn't mean that I can hold others to my standard.

My assistant's lateness does not reflect on me.

Alternative belief:

An occasional lateness is more manageable than I originally thought.

Education

Education is another strategy to change beliefs. Education is a way to examine and challenge perfectionism beliefs. Seeking accurate and current information on a given topic can alter rigid beliefs by providing evidence to refute or support it. Education includes the willingness to examine the evidence that will either confirm or contradict your beliefs. For example, if you believe that drastically changing a product is the only way the organization will survive, rather than making this change based on assuming that your prediction is true; examine the evidence. Have there been complaints about the product, what changes if any have your competitors made, would the change enhance the products marketability, etc? Utilize your plan for change as a guide to employ this strategy to your identified beliefs.

Hypothesis Testing

Another effective strategy to change perfectionism beliefs is hypothesis testing. That is, testing the validity of your beliefs by conducting experiments. Hypothesis testing will provide you with valuable information by proving or disproving your belief. Use your plan for change to design experiments to prove or disprove your beliefs. Record your experiments and findings in a journal.

Example

Experiment: Arrive late for the next executive meeting

Belief/predicted outcome: People will be angry and I will lose face.

Actual outcome: No one on the executive team expressed or displayed angry. In fact, they all spoke to me in a pleasant, professional and respectful manner.

Changing Behaviors

This section discusses and demonstrates employing the strategy of exposure to change the behaviors of perfectionism.

Perfectionism behaviors help to maintain maladaptive beliefs and attitudes. You can not disprove or challenge your beliefs if you continually engage in maladaptive behaviors. For example, if you believe that everyone should arrive fifteen minutes before a meeting to maintain your high standards, the act of always showing up fifteen minutes early prevents you from ever finding out if you belief is true. Therefore, changing behaviors will also change beliefs by providing new learning experiences.

Exposure

The strategy of exposure consists of creating practice or confronting situations which cause maladaptive behaviors to decrease the fear of failure associated with them. For example, you recheck your work several times before you hand it in, fearing humiliation/failure. You create an 'imperfect' situation where you check your work only once before turning it in. Repeated exposures to the 'imperfect' situation will decrease the anxiety and fear you usually feel; which causes you to check your work several times before turning it in. You should continue the controlled exposures until the behavior is no longer a problem.

The exposure strategy works best when it is under your control, and spaced close together for an extended period of time. For example, if you are anxious about speaking before a group, making a presentation once a month may never reduce your fear. However, if you expose yourself to public speaking everyday for two weeks you will notice a substantial decrease in your anxiety/fear.

You will feel discomfort during the practice exposures, this is normal. This discomfort is the worst thing that will happen during the controlled exposure. A decrease in this discomfort level is an indication that the behavior is changing and therefore should be monitored.

Begin an exposure journal that documents the behavior, the situation and the level of anxiety experienced as well as indicate the number of times you have been exposed to that particular situation. Use an anxiety scale from 0 to 10 to monitor the exposure discomfort level. For example, 0 = no anxiety, 5 = moderate anxiety and 10 = great anxiety.

Start with exposure to easy situations and work your way up to more difficult situations at a comfortable pace for you. Utilize your plan for change to identify the perfectionism behaviors to begin to plan the 'imperfect' situations.

Example
Behavior: I cannot stand it when all my papers are not filed by the end of the day.
Belief: I must be organized to be successful.
Exposure: Leave papers on my desk at the end of each day.
Number of exposure: 4th
Anxiety level: 5

Professional Help

If you find that the exercises are too difficult for you it is an indication that your perfectionism behaviors and beliefs are too rigid to change by yourself. This is an indication that you need to seek the help of a trained professional. Seeking the help of a mental health professional is recommended for everyone who has identified maladaptive perfectionism as a real or potential problem. A mental health professional will be able to explain concepts and walk you though the exercises as well facilitate and employ strategies not included in this book.

In addition, the web site for the National Institute of Mental Health (www.nimh.nih.gov) is a good reference for additional information about available treatments and referrals.

Tale of the Perfect Dam Leader – Week Six

Malaper and his workers arrived early to survey the strong and sturdy dam they had constructed over the Macpan River. The workers had overcome the unrealistic expectations and the delays caused by Malaper's excessive attention to detail and successfully completed the dam. They had been successful in spite of the dam leader and experienced a sense of personal pleasure at their accomplishment.

The Grand Wizard and his advisors surveyed the completed project and were pleased and impressed by Malper's dam. They congratulated and praised Malaper for the excellent job. Malaper accepted the praise feeling on one hand that he certainly deserved to be praised and on the other hand that the Grand Wizard and his advisors were mocking him. He assured the Grand Wizard that if awarded the construction project he would keep tighter reins on the workers to meet the deadline.

The Grand Wizard smiled, nodded and left. Malaper returned to his office planning on reorganizing the papers on his desk. The team members also left the site, some were so fatigued that they would call out sick tomorrow, some would start looking for another job and some would return to the status quo of the Malaper Construction Company.

The Grand Wizard and his advisors met and discussed the project, the dams and the dam leaders and reached a decision on who should be awarded the contract to construct dams throughout the Kingdom.

Who do you think was awarded the contract?

References

Antony, M.M. & Swinson, R.P. (1998). When Perfect Isn't Good Enough: Strategies for Coping with Perfectionism. New Harbinger Press.

Bandura, A. (1997). Self-Efficacy: The Exercise of Control. New York: W.H. Freeman and Company.

Bandura, A. (1986). Social Foundations of Thought & Action: A Social Cognitive Theory. Upper Saddle River, New Jersey: Prentice Hall.

Basco, M. R. (1999). Never Good Enough: How to Use Perfectionism to Your Advantage Without Letting it Ruin Your Life. New York: Simon & Schuster.

Chen, C., Gully, S. & Eden, D. (2001). Validation of a new general self-efficacy scale. Organizational research Methods, 4 (1), 62-83.

Chesterton, G.K. (1910). What's Wrong with the World. Ignatius

Ciaramicoli. A.P. (2004). Performance Addiction: The Dangerous New Syndrome and How to Stop It from Ruining Your Life. John Wiley & Sons, Inc.

Curan, C. (1999). The Care and Feeding of Perfectionists. Georgetown, Massachusetts: North Star Publications.

Downs, A. (1997). Beyond The Looking Glass. New York : AMACOM

Ellis, A. (1957). How to Live with a "Neurotic" at Home and at Work. No. Hollywood, CA: Melvin Powers Wilshire Book Company.

Flett, G.L. & Hewitt, P.L. (2002). Perfectionism: Theory, Research and Treatment. Washington, D.C.: American Psychological Association.

Frost, R.O, Martin, P., Lahart, C. & Rosenblate, R. (1990). The dimensions of perfectionism. Cognitive Therapy and Research, 14, 449-468.

Goleman, D., Botatzis, R. & McKee, A. (2002). Primal Leadership: Realizing the Power of Emotional Intelligence. Boston, Massachusetts: Harvard Business School Press.

Herman, G. (1999). Slip! Slide! Skate! New York: Scholastic Inc.

King, J. (2003). Perfectionism in Leadership: Exploring the link between Leader Self- Esteem, Leader Self-Efficacy, Leader-Narcissism and Perfectionism. Doctoral dissertation. Regent University

Lasch, C. (1979). The Culture of Narcissism: American Life in an Age of Diminishing Expectations. New York: W. W. Norton & Company.

Maccaby, M. (2003). The Productive Narcissist: The Promise and Peril of Visionary Leadership. New York: Broadway Books.

Mallinger, A.E. & DeWyze, J. (1992). Too Perfect: When Being in Control Gets Out of Control. New York: Fawcett Books.

McFarlin, D. & Sweeney, D. (2000). House of Mirrors: The Untold Truth about Narcissistic Leaders and How to Survive Them. Kogan Page.

Miller, J. (1997). Egotopia: Narcissism and the New American Landscape. Tuscaloosa: The University of Alabama Press.

Raskin, R. & Terry, H. (1998). A principal-components analysis of the narcissistic personality inventory and further evidence of its construct validity. Journal of Personality and Social Psychology, 54 (5), 890-902.

Rosenberg, M. (1965). Society and the Adolescent Self-Image. New Jersey: Princeton University Press.

Rothstein, A. (1984). The Narcissistic Pursuit of Perfection. New York: International University Press, Inc.

Schiraldi, G.R. (2001). The Self-Esteem Workbook. New Harbinger Publications, Inc.

Smith, A. W. (1990). Overcoming Perfectionism: The Key to a Balanced Recovery. Deerfield Beach, Florida: Health Communications, Inc.

Sorensen, M. J. (2002). The Personal Workbook for Breaking the Chain of Low Self- Esteem: A Proven Program for Recovery from LSE. Sherwood, OR: Wolf Publishing Co.